ALFRISTON CLERGY HOUSE

East Sussex

The National Trust

Alfriston Clergy House

The projecting north-east corner of the house

The Clergy House *c.*1820; detail from a pencil drawing by Edward Blore (British Library)

'Tiny but beautiful, with orchard and a sweep of lowland river behind it.' So the Clergy House was described in the 1890s by Octavia Hill, one of the three founders of the National Trust. It stands on the outskirts of the South Downs village of Alfriston beside the Tye, or village green, and between the fourteenth-century St Andrew's church and the Cuckmere river.

The Clergy House may have been built as early as 1350, in the aftermath of the Black Death, which struck Britain in 1348. Out of a population of four million people, around one and a half million died from this strain of bubonic plague in the first two years; it killed eight of the thirteen Augustinian canons at nearby Michelham Priory. Half the land was left untilled, and manor houses were ruined or abandoned. Latin graffiti scrawled on a church in Hertfordshire sum up the desperate mood of those left alive: '1350, wretched, wild, distracted. The dregs of the mob alone survive to tell the tale'. It took decades for the economy to recover, but when it did, building began again with renewed flourish. The Clergy House was probably built by a yeoman farmer who had prospered in this stricken land. In the fifteenth century it passed into the possession of Michelham Priory, and remained church property for the next five centuries.

When the Church Commissioners visited Alfriston in the early eighteenth century, they found the building 'in good repair'. However, by the late nineteenth century it was practically derelict, and demolition was proposed. It is almost entirely thanks to one man, the local vicar, the Rev. F.W.Beynon, that the Clergy House survived. He set up an appeal to save this ancient building, and then in 1896 arranged its sale to the fledgling National Trust for a token £10. The Clergy House was the first historic building acquired by the Trust, and the first that it restored. From these modest beginnings has grown all the Trust's work with historic buildings large and small over the past 100 years.

The tile-hung west end of the house

The Building

Alfriston Clergy House is typical of many thousands of timber-framed 'Wealden' houses put up during the late Middle Ages, predominantly in Kent and Sussex. The oak frame was filled in with interwoven strips of chestnut or oak, which were covered with daub and finally limewashed. It consists of two storeys, set under a single expanse of roof hipped at both ends, with the upper storey at the east end 'jettied out' (projecting) on the overhanging ends of the floor beams. For Octavia Hill, such picturesque houses were 'rich in memories of England as our ancestors knew it', but structurally they were very forward-looking, embodying the principles that underlie the steel-framed, box-girder buildings of today.

The plan is simplicity itself: a central, communal hall open to the rafters, flanked to the east by the family rooms, a parlour and lavatory (garderobe) placed conveniently on the south-east corner, with a solar (living-room) on the floor above; at the opposite end were two floors of humbler service rooms, where food would have been prepared and stored, and the servants slept above.

In the mid-sixteenth century the western, service end, which was also once jettied, was demolished and replaced by a new cross-wing of two bays, which projected to the rear. The addition is seen most clearly on the north-facing entrance front, where the 'close studding' (closely grouped vertical timbers) of the new work at the west end contrasts with the diagonal foot and head bracing in the central and eastern sections. The parlour was moved to the new west wing, which had stairs up to two chambers above, and was warmed by fireplaces connected to a new single brick chimneystack against the west end of the building. By the 1550s chilly open halls were becoming unfashionable in Wealden houses, and around this date many were divided horizontally by inserting a new floor. This is what happened at Alfriston, where a new fireplace was also placed against the rear wall.

Many of the original window openings have survived, but they were not filled with glass until about 1600; before that shutters or cloth would have been all that kept out the weather. In the middle of the eighteenth century the rear part of the west crosswing was replaced by a single-storey lean-to that runs along the rear of the house. As the building gradually declined in status later in the century, it was divided into two cottages. It may also have been around this date that the roof was thatched.

The entrance front

The Interior

The house is entered through the garden door at the back of the building, which leads into a small room that is part of the mid-eighteenth-century lean-to. In the far left-hand corner can be seen an exposed section of the original outside wall showing the wattle and daub infill. The laths were split rather than sawn and woven when still green, a technique still used for wattle fencing panels today. The steps opposite the door lead into the mid-sixteenth-century west wing.

The Parlour

This was the principal family room of the house in the sixteenth century. In the original building it contained the service quarters and formed two rooms, the pantry and buttery, each opening on to the Hall – hence the two doorways. A staircase would have led to the rooms above, which served either as additional accommodation and storage space or as the servants' quarters.

In the left-hand corner of the fireplace is a bread oven. After this had been heated with faggots, dough would be placed inside with a peel, a long-handled shovel made out of wood or iron. The furniture is all seventeenth-century and is made of English oak, apart from the pair of benches, which are chestnut and probably French.

The Hall

This is the centre of the building and its communal focus, where the yeoman farmer, his family and servants would have eaten. Today it again rises through two storeys to the rafters, although the positions of the joists that supported the first floor (removed in 1896) can still be seen. The roof is supported on timbers that incorporate a central vertical 'crown-post' which gives its name to this kind of construction. The crossbeams that form the inner walls at the east and west ends are finely moulded, and in the north-east corner the point at which they meet is carved in the form of an oak leaf.

Remains of the first hearth have been discovered beneath the floor in the centre of the room. Smoke from this open fire would have escaped through the windows and through the roof, where soot-blackened timbers can still be seen. The air did not become clearer until a fireplace was inserted against the south wall in the mid-sixteenth century (removed in 1896).

The carved oakleaf decoration in the Hall

The west end of the Hall, with the Parlour beyond

The east end of the Hall. The floor is a traditional Sussex feature, made from lumps of local chalk rammed down and sealed with sour milk. It has recently been relaid

7

The Garden

Set in approximately two-thirds of an acre, this cottage garden continues to mature within the framework conceived in the 1920s by Sir Robert Witt, who was the tenant at that time. The front garden is filled with traditional 'cottage' favourites, some grown since Roman times and including rarities now almost lost to cultivation.

A feature of the garden is the Judas Tree (*Cercis siliquastrum*), which was damaged in the 1987 hurricane but is still a sea of pink, pea-like flowers in early June. Behind it lies the orchard, cut as a hay meadow and home to some important spring wild flowers.

The back garden is terraced on three levels. The door is wreathed with scented climbing roses, honeysuckle and clematis, mixed with aromatic herbs nearly smothered by a rampant perennial pea. The roses in the borders have been chosen for their perfume and are underplanted with campanulas, herbaceous geraniums and other cottage favourites, as are the shop and shrub borders.

There is also a small herb garden, containing a wide variety of cooking, strewing and medicinal plants; more herbs can be found in the topiary garden. Here four magnificent clipped box trees are underplanted with old laced pinks in beds divided by a sundial.

The porch is smothered with a mixture of *Rosa multiflora*, *Clematis* 'Comtesse du Bouchaud' and the perennial sweet pea *Lathyrus rotundifolius*

The kitchen garden is laid out in *potager* style with raised beds edged with herbs, in which are grown artichokes, broad beans, Brussels sprouts and a variety of other vegetables and flowers for cutting

The terraced back garden

The Clergy House in Danger

The Clergy House around 1858

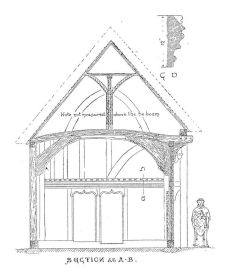

SECTION AB A·B.

Beynon commissioned a London architect, Henry Stock, to survey the building in October 1894

The Rev. F.W. Beynon began the repair of the derelict Clergy House by putting up a roof of matchboarding in 1893

As the Clergy House was church property, the responsibility for its upkeep fell on the vicar of St Andrew's. By 1885 it had fallen into such a dilapidated state that he applied to the Ecclesiastical Commissioners for permission to demolish the building and sell the materials. To this they agreed. However, the occupant, an old woman who had been born and spent her life there, pleaded with the vicar to be allowed to end her days in the Clergy House. He must have agreed, as demolition was deferred, and she continued to live in the house until her death in 1888. The following year the Rev. F.W. Beynon was appointed to the living of St Andrew's.

In the 1890s there was a growing interest in the ancient vernacular buildings of Britain, inspired by books like Ralph Nevill's *Old English Cottage and Domestic Architecture in South West Surrey* (1889). Beynon, who was a member of the Sussex Archaeological Society, quickly realised that the Clergy House was an important relic of medieval England. For seven years he sought to save the building. He turned to the Sussex Archaeological Society for technical advice, and then to the Society for the Protection of Ancient Buildings (SPAB) in London. Both were encouraging, but could not provide the money to pay for the urgently needed repairs.

In August 1892 Beynon launched an appeal for £450, to repair the building and convert it for use as a reading room and for other parochial purposes. He had the backing of both societies and a long list of famous names headed by the Dukes of Norfolk, Devonshire and Newcastle 'who expressed their cordial sympathy and offered assistance'. However, by February 1893 the appeal had produced only £124. This enabled the Vicar to call in a London architect and builder, who made a start on the most essential work, putting up a roof of matchboarding over the east end where the gaping holes in the thatch let in every shower. Nevertheless, the building remained in a perilous state.

In July 1894 the SPAB advised Beynon to approach the 'National Trust for Places of Historic Interest or Natural Beauty', which had been formed only ten days before.

The National Trust and the Clergy House

The Clergy House from the south-east

The old barn, which once stood next to the Clergy House but has since gone

The Clergy House was exactly the kind of ancient and humble building that the National Trust, inspired by the example of John Ruskin and William Morris, had been set up to save. Octavia Hill took an immediate interest. She wrote to Sydney Cockerell of the SPAB of 'the pleading voice of the old building itself, which I am sure you hear as clearly as I do pleading to be left to tell its story to the days that are to come.' After complicated negotiations, the Ecclesiastical Commissioners agreed to sell the Clergy House on 16 April 1896 for a nominal £10 to the National Trust – its first building and second property.

This was only the first stage; Octavia Hill agreed that they would have to 'restore it, in so far as that odious word means preservation from decay', but she was adamant: 'Into a safe state it must be got'. The vital thing was to find the right architect, 'whose heart was in the matter and who could decide point by point on the spot what to do, and see to its being done, with knowledge of art and craft'. The man chosen was Alfred Powell, who had produced pamphlets for the SPAB on the repair of country buildings.

But first the money for repairs had to be found. On 15 June 1896, in a letter to *The Times* and *Standard*, the Trust made its first public appeal for funds. The sum required was £350 – tiny by today's standards, but in 1900 the Trust's entire annual income was only £300, and Octavia Hill was determined that it should live within its means. In August 1896 she wrote to the Rev. B.H.Alford, who had made a donation to the appeal:

We really must put the repairs in hand this summer or the whole building will be lost, and I cannot begin the habit of ordering work for which I have not the money. We are to have a Com[mitt]ee tomorrow, and I am going to propose to put the roof in hand, and to get the cottage end so repaired as to let us put in a caretaker, which is also urgent. If we have got enough to do this by tomorrow all will be well. [The failure of the appeal] would be not only a loss of some valuable possession for our country for all time, but a sort of breach of trust so far as Alfriston is concerned because it is our's now, given in the expectation we could preserve it. Besides all this hope is a great factor inspiring people to work and gift, and if our Nat. Trust failed in these small schemes in this the opening work, it would throw back the future work.

The National Trust

FOR PLACES OF HISTORIC INTEREST OR NATURAL BEAUTY,

1, GREAT COLLEGE STREET, WESTMINSTER, S.W.

APPEAL FOR THE PRESERVATION OF THE PRE-REFORMATION CLERGY HOUSE, ALFRISTON, SUSSEX.

This very interesting relic of the Middle Ages, situate in a secluded Sussex village, at the foot of the South Downs, has been made over to the National Trust, by the Vicar and the Ecclesiastical Commissioners, for the nominal sum of £10. The building is one both of interest and of beauty, and is much visited by persons staying at Eastbourne and Seaford, both within a drive.

The Clergy House Preserved

Octavia Hill, one of the founders of the National Trust, played an important part in saving the Clergy House; painting after J. S. Sargent

Robert and Mary Witt and their son John at Alfriston around 1909. The Witts were the Trust's first tenants of the Clergy House

There were sufficient funds for Powell to make a start on repairing the Clergy House. He took down the wooden roof over the east end of the building, replacing it with new thatch. The rear wall had to be almost entirely renewed, and he removed the floor and fireplace from the central hall to return it to its original fifteenth-century appearance. But otherwise he was scrupulous in altering the building as little as possible, in accordance with the best SPAB principles. Money came in slowly, but by July 1898 enough had been raised to complete the works, thanks to a donation of £50 by the Duke of Devonshire, a member of the Trust's Council. In all the appeal raised £184 19s, including an anonymous donation of 6d, the rest being found from the Trust's sparse general funds.

Until 1974 the Clergy House was let to a series of tenants who paid for the upkeep and opened the Hall to visitors. The Arts and Crafts movement architect C. R. Ashbee spent his honeymoon here in September 1898, arranging red apples along the beams of the Hall and swimming in the nearby Cuckmere river. The first tenant was Sir Robert Witt, the founder of the Witt Photographic Library, who used the house as a weekend cottage. In 1977, after another campaign of repairs, the Trust took over the running of the house, and the whole of the ground floor and the garden were opened to visitors for the first time.

In September 1898 Mr Beynon died in office, burdened by debts incurred in rescuing the Clergy House. He was buried in the churchyard of St Andrew's next to the building he had done so much to preserve. In 1896 he had written to the *Daily Chronicle*:

From the first day I saw it seven years ago until the day it passed into the hands of the National Trust it was my constant care and anxiety. . . . No mother could have shown more unwearied solicitude for her first-born darling than I bestowed on it day and night. . . . I would conclude by saying that not a shilling has been given inside the parish to preserve the building, whilst Noah when building his ark could scarcely have been subjected to more open scorn and silent contempt for what was regarded as my hobby and my folly.

It is on the efforts of such indefatigable campaigners that the success of the National Trust has been built.